MY FIRST ENCYCLOPEDIA

An eye-catching series of information books designed to encourage young children to find out more about the world around them. Each one is carefully prepared by a subject specialist with the help of experienced writers and educational advisers.

KINGFISHER
Kingfisher Publications Plc
New Penderel House, 283-288 High Holborn, London WC1V 7HZ

First published in paperback by Kingfisher Publications Plc 1994
2 4 6 8 10 9 7 5 3
2TR/1BP/0600/SF/(FR)/135MA

Originally published in hardback under the series title Young World
This edition © copyright Kingfisher Publications Plc 2000
Text & Illustrations © copyright Kingfisher Publications Plc 1992

ISBN 1 85697 266 6

Phototypeset by Waveney Typesetters, Norwich
Printed in China

MY FIRST ENCYCLOPEDIA

The Sea

Kingfisher

Author
Nina Morgan

Natural history consultant
Michael Chinery

Educational consultant
Daphne Ingram

Series consultant
Brian Williams

Editor
Camilla Hallinan

Designer
Tony Potter, Times Four Publishing

Illustrators
John Barber (pages 12-13, 16-17, 18-19, 22-23,
26-29 & 40)
Bob Corley (30-31, 38-39, 46-47, 50-53 & 62-63)
Peter Dennis (15, 43, 72, 92-102 & 106-119)
Terry Hadler (17, 22, 42 & 44-47)
David Kearney (103)
Swanston Graphics (12, 14-15, 18-19, 22-25, 40-41,
86-87 & 118-19)
Treve Tamblin (32-35, 54-61, 64-67 & 70-89)

About this book

Have you ever stood on the beach and wondered how big the sea is? If you were out in Space and you looked down at the Earth, you would see that seas and oceans cover most of our planet. This book shows how important they are.

The sea helps to control the world's climate. It also helps to shape the coastline, whether there is a towering cliff or a flat, soggy marsh. The sea provides a home for millions of plants and animals. It is also full of valuable resources – food, oil, salt and many other things we use every day.

From the tiny grains of sand on the beach to the dramatic mountains and valleys hidden deep beneath the water, the sea is a fascinating place. But people are damaging the sea, and it needs your help. With this book, you can begin to find out more about the sea. Only by finding out more can we all learn how to use the sea more wisely.

CONTENTS

COASTLINES

THE OPEN SEA

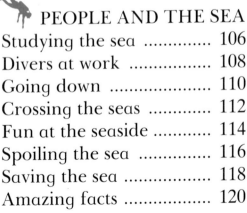

OCEAN RICHES

PEOPLE AND THE SEA

World of

water

🌍 Our blue planet

If you looked down at the Earth from Space, you would see that most of our planet is covered by the ocean.

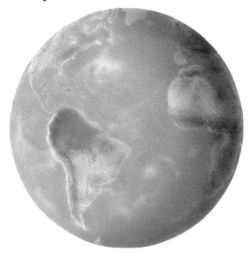

More than 70 per cent of the Earth is covere in water.

Life began in the ocean about 3,500 million years ago. Tiny plants produced a gas called oxygen. Oxygen made it possible for other forms of life to develop.

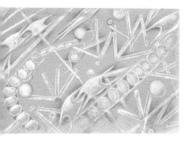

plankton

Now the ocean is home to millions of plants and animals – from tiny plankton to huge blue whales.

 Oceans and seas

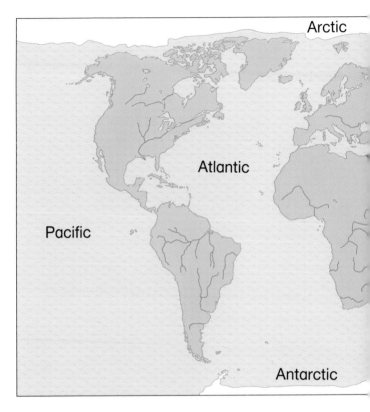

There is really only one ocean on the
Earth. This huge ocean is separated into
five smaller oceans by the continents.
The five oceans are the Pacific, Atlantic,
Indian, Arctic and Antarctic Oceans.

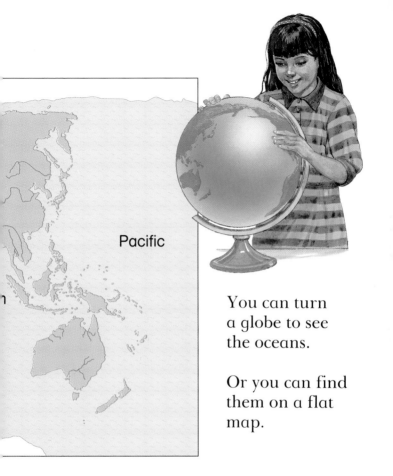

Pacific

You can turn
a globe to see
the oceans.

Or you can find
them on a flat
map.

¹s are parts of the oceans. The
editerranean, the Bering Sea and the
ribbean are the largest seas, but there
² also many others. (Sometimes people
³ "sea" when they mean "ocean".)

 Seawater

If you have ever swum in the sea and tasted seawater, you will know that it is salty. Seawater is salty because it contain salts and minerals from rocks.

fresh water   seawater

Some salts and minerals are dissolved fro rocks on the seafloor. Others are carried into the sea from rocks on land, by strean and rivers. River water does not taste salty. It is called fresh water.

lt helps you float when you swim in the a. Some parts of the oceans are very salty. he saltiest water is in the Dead Sea tween Israel and Jordan. But it is not a a at all. It is a lake.

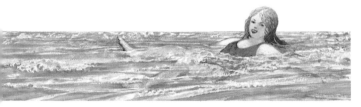

he least salty part of the oceans is in the lantic Ocean, off South America. There, e Amazon River pours illions of litres of esh water into e ocean.

🌍 Warm water, cold wat

Sunlight heats the water near
the surface of the sea.

In the tropics around the
Equator, the sun shines for
many hours each day.
So the sea is warm
enough to swim in
all the year round.

Less sunlight shines on the
oceans around the North
and South Poles.

South Pole

In the Arctic and
Antarctic Oceans
around the poles, the
water is so cold that
it freezes. The huge
pieces of floating ice
are called ice floes or
ice packs.

polar sea

North Pole

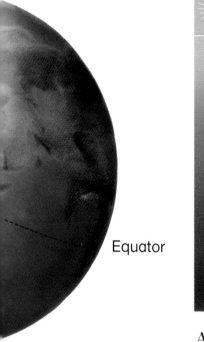

Equator

All seawater is
cold deep down.
Cold water is
heavier than
warm water, so
it sinks to the
bottom. Sunlight
cannot reach that
far down.

pical sea

Amazing facts

🌎 Ninety-seven per cent of all the water on the Earth is in the oceans.

🌎 The Pacific is the biggest ocean, and the deepest. The Arctic is the smallest ocean, and the shallowest.

🌎 The coldest sea surface temperature minus two degrees Celsius. That is in the White Sea, in the Arctic Ocean.

🌎 The warmest sea surface temperatur is 35.6 degrees Celsius. This occurs in the summer, in shallow parts of the Persian Gulf in the Indian Ocean.

🌎 Some ice floes are so big that people live on them. Russian scientists once buil a research station on a huge ice floe in the Antarctic. After several years they h to leave because the ice began to melt.

A changing

world

 # The changing world

The surface of the Earth is a thin shell of rock called the crust. The crust is made up of 13 huge pieces called plates.

Hot, soft rock flows up from inside the Earth and pushes these plates around. This movement is called plate tectonics.

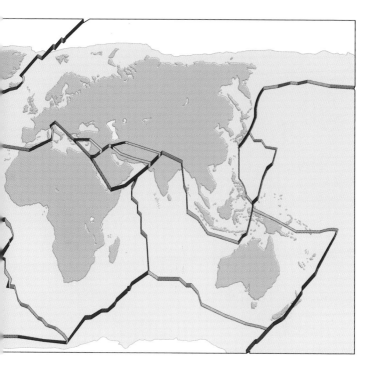

Some parts of the Earth's surface move
as much as 20 centimetres every year.
The movement of the plates means
the continents and oceans are
slowly changing shape
all the time.

Pangaea

200 million years ago

Two hundred million years ago there was only one continent, called Pangaea (pan-gee-ah).

Pangaea was surrounded by a single ocean.

Currents of hot soft rock came up from inside the Earth. Little by little, they opened up large cracks in the land. Pieces of Pangaea split off and drifted apart to form new continents.

65 million years ago

olten or liquid rock
elled up and
rmed new seafloor
the gaps. Water
owed in and
rmed new oceans.

Many islands were once part of continents. They broke away when the seafloor split apart.

Madagascar broke away from Africa.

today

he size and shape of the oceans are still
nanging. The Atlantic Ocean is growing
bout four centimetres wider every year.
he Pacific Ocean is becoming narrower.

 # The ocean floor

At the edge of each continent, the land forms a shallow shelf under the sea. The edge of the shelf slopes steeply down to th seafloor. The large flat areas on the seafloor are called abyssal plains.

But the seafloor is not flat everywhere.

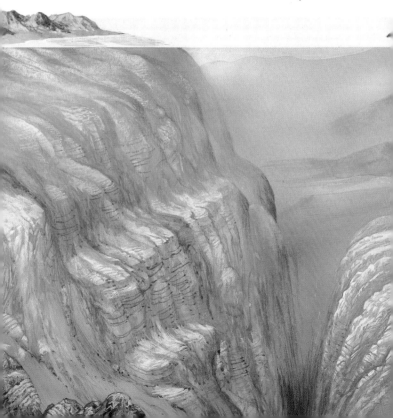

some places, the seafloor is covered with
small extinct volcanoes called abyssal hills.
There are also towering mountains called
seamounts – they were made by large
volcanoes. And there are deep gorges
called trenches. Underwater landscape is
as dramatic as the Grand Canyon!

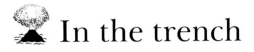 # In the trench

Trenches are deep, narrow valleys. It is pitch dark in the trenches, because sunlig[ht] cannot reach the bottom. Most trenches are in the Pacific Ocean. The deepest is the Marianas Trench, near Japan.

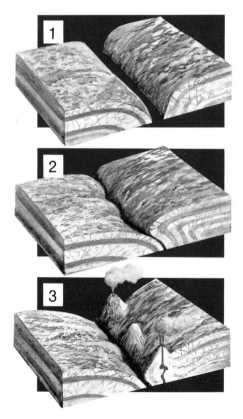

When two plate[s] in the Earth's crust collide, on[e] plate is pushed below the other. The gap betwee[n] them forms a trench. This takes thousands of years.

Both plates are under pressure. So earthquakes and volcanic eruptions occur.

The Marianas Trench is 11 kilometres deep. If you dropped Mount Everest in the trench, the mountain's peak would not reach the surface.

surface

Mount Everest

two
kilometres
deep

eleven
kilometres
deep

 # Underwater mountair

The longest mountain chains on Earth ar
under water. They are called the mid-
ocean ridges. This is how they form.

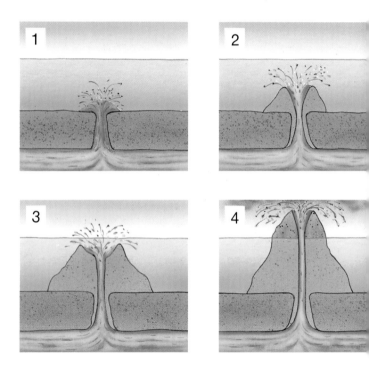

When plates move apart, molten rock wel
up. It hardens into ridges. As more molt
rock wells up, the ridges grow higher.

ome parts of the ridges poke through the
cean surface and make new islands.

ew islands are also formed when
nderwater volcanoes erupt.

fter each eruption, volcanic lava forms a
ew layer of rock. Eventually the volcano
rows tall enough to reach the surface.

Coral islands

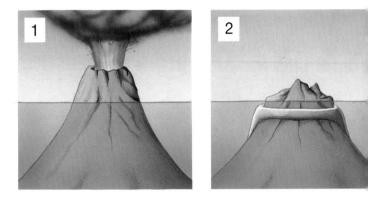

When an island emerges in warm parts of
the world, tiny animals called corals may
come to live in the warm, shallow water
around the island. The corals build a reef
on the sides of the island. The reef is home
to masses of colourful plants and animals.

Over thousands of years, the island may
begin to sink. The corals build upwards,
to stay in warm, shallow water. After the
island sinks below the surface, all that can
be seen above is a ring of coral reef called
an atoll. The water inside the atoll forms
a lagoon.

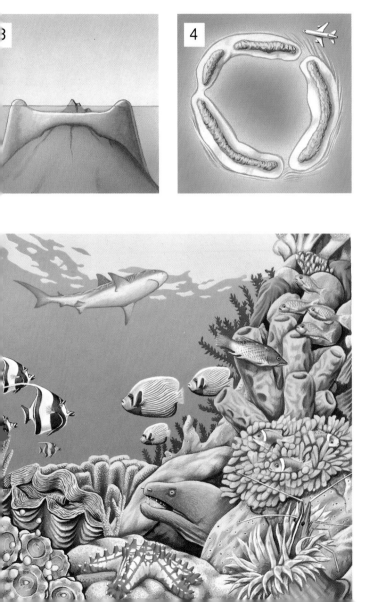

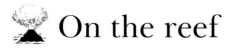 On the reef

It takes millions of corals to build a reef. Even a small piece of coral is made of hundreds of tiny animals. They start life as buds growing on their parents. Each animal has a hard limestone shell.

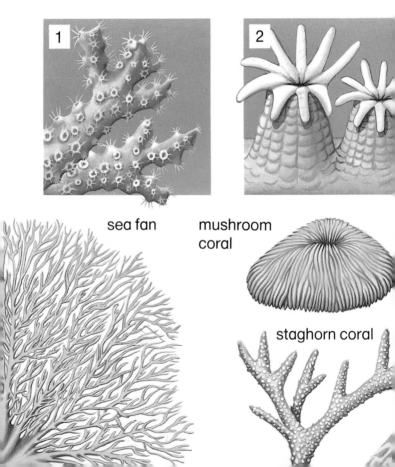

sea fan

mushroom coral

staghorn coral

When corals die, new corals build on top of their shells. The layers of coral form walls of limestone. These walls are the reefs.

Many types of animals and plants live in and around coral reefs, because they can find a safe place to live and plenty to eat.

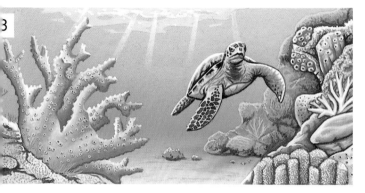

orange
cup coral

The crown-of-thorns starfish eats coral. These animals can kill a coral reef in just a few months.

brain coral

Amazing facts

The highest underwater mountain is in the Pacific, between Samoa and New Zealand. It is 8.7 kilometres high. That is nearly as tall as Mount Everest, the world's highest mountain.

Iceland is made up of the tops of some of the volcanoes in the mid-Atlantic ridge.

Greenland is the largest island. It was once part of the North American continent.

One of the newest islands is Lateika, in the Pacific. This island was formed when a volcano erupted in the 1970s.

The longest coral reef is the Great Barrier Reef, in the Pacific. This stretches for over 2,000 kilometres along the north-eastern coast of Australia.

Wind and

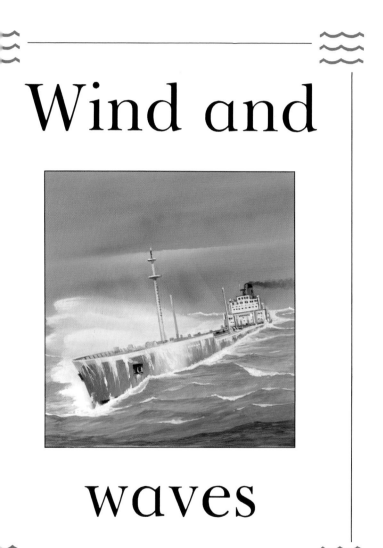

waves

≋ Oceans and weather

The oceans help to control the climate.
They do this by soaking up heat from the
Sun during the day, and by releasing it
very slowly at night.

The oceans are also an important part of
the water cycle.

In the cycle, the Sun's heat turns some
seawater into an invisible gas called water
vapour. The vapour rises into the air.
When it reaches cold air, the vapour turn
into tiny drops of water.

The drops of water join together and make clouds. The water in the clouds falls as rain, snow or hail. Most of it falls into the oceans. But even when it falls on land, the water eventually flows back into the oceans.

≈ Ocean currents

Currents are like huge rivers in the ocean.
They carry water from one part of the
world to another. Some currents flow near
the surface. Icebergs drift on surface
currents around the poles. Other currents
flow deep down, along the seafloor.

There are many
surface currents.
Some are warm
and some are cold.
They link up and
make six large
loops called gyres.

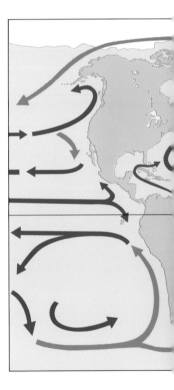

rong winds in the tropics around the
quator push the surface currents from
st to west. Near the poles, winds push
e currents back round again.

s the winds push them along, the currents
nd around the continents and change
rection.

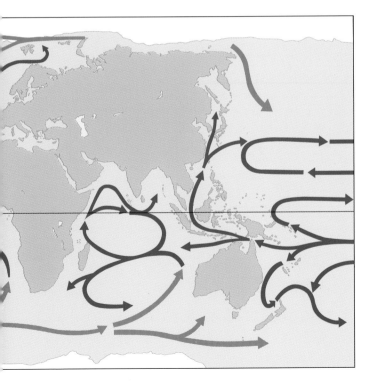

≋ Waves

Waves are made by wind blowing across the ocean. Water in the waves seems to move forwards, but really the water move up and around and down.

The top of the wave is called the crest, an the bottom is called the trough.

When waves reach the shore they break. Waves break because water at the bottom catches on the seabed, while water on the crest keeps moving forward.

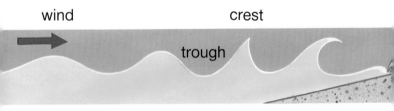

wind   crest

trough

Surfers like high waves. These occur whe strong winds blow for days across wide stretches of ocean. The highest waves are found in the biggest ocean, the Pacific.

≋ Stormy seas

In a storm, strong winds blow across the surface of the sea. As the winds blow, they whip up huge waves with ragged foamy edges. This kind of wave is called a whitecap. In really violent storms, whitecaps can be more than 15 metres high.

he most dangerous waves are tsunamis.
hese waves are started by underwater
rthquakes and volcanic eruptions. Out
 sea, tsunamis are low. But when a
unami reaches land, it rears up to a huge
eight and crashes down with great force.
 tsunami can cause terrible damage.

≋ The tides

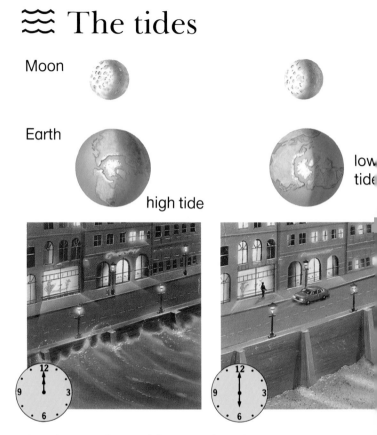

Moon

Earth

high tide

low tide

Twice a day, tides make the oceans' wate
level rise and fall. During a high tide, the
water moves farther onto the land. Durir
a low tide, the water moves back.

What causes tides? The Moon's pull, and
the Earth's spin.

n the side of the globe facing the Moon,
e Moon's gravity pulls the oceans.

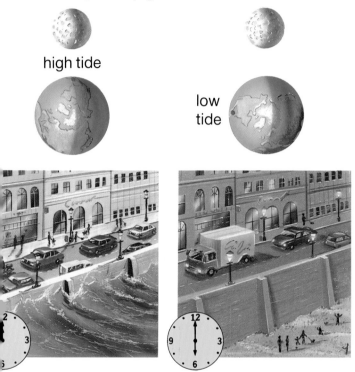

high tide

low
tide

n the other side of the globe, the Moon's
avity pulls the Earth away from the
eans. So both places have high tides.

ery 24 hours the Earth spins right
ound. So most coasts have two high tides
day. Follow the red dot to see why.

47

Amazing facts

≈ The Gulf Stream is a current that brings warm water from the tropics all the way up the Atlantic to Ireland and Britain.

≈ The highest tsunami was 525 metres high. It started in the Pacific Ocean and hit land in Lituya Bay in Alaska, in 1958.

≈ The highest tides in the world occur in the Atlantic Ocean, in the Bay of Fundy in Canada. Here, the difference between low and high tides is more than 16 metres.

≈ Extra-high high tides tides occur when the Moon is between the Earth and the Sun. Then the Sun and the Moon both pull on the oceans. These tides are called spring tides.

Coastlines

🐚 Along the coast

Coastlines are where the land meets the s
Some coastlines are formed as a result of
erosion. Erosion takes place when wind c
waves beat against the land and break it

bay

cliff

headl

Erosion goes on all the time, so the shape
of a coastline is always changing.

metimes the waves wear away soft rock
 the cliff. This forms a bay.
he harder rock may be left sticking out as
peninsula or headland. Sometimes part
 the headland is worn right through to
rm stacks and arches.

ve
arch
stack

nd on some coastlines, waves carve out
ves at the bottom of the cliffs.

Sand and shingle

Sand is made by erosion. Waves wash ove
boulders of rock and rub them against on
another. This slowly breaks them up.

The pieces of boulder are worn down int
small pebbles, then gravel, and finally tin
grains of sand.

eaches form where the waves drop sand
nd gravel and other sediment onto the
ore. If the waves and currents are very
rong, they carry away the sand and leave
st the gravel, pebbles or boulders.

each sediments are always on the move.
aves and currents move them along the
ast or into deeper water.

🐚 Nesting in the cliffs

The coastline is home to many plants and animals.

Puffins, gannets and guillemots all nest o cliffs. They live close to one another, but each has its own territory.

Puffins build their nests in burrows at the top of the cliff. Gannets make nests out of seaweed. Guillemots don't build nests at a They simply lay their eggs on a rocky ledg

These seabirds don't have to go far to fin their food. The sea provides plenty of fis and plankton to eat. The birds use rising currents of warm air to soar up from the water and back to their nesting sites.

🐚 The water's edge

Animals and plants which live on a rocky shore lead a double life. When the tide is in, they must live under water. When the tide is out, they must survive in the air.

Barnacles and mussels live on the rocks. When the tide is in, these animals open their shells and stick out their feathery legs, to catch plankton. Plankton are too small to see, but the water is full of them.

nails and limpets come out of their shells
and graze on the seaweed growing on the
rocks. Starfish feed on the snails and the
mussels. Crabs hunt for food too – they eat
almost anything! Prawns, anemones and
small fish live in pools which do not dry up.

When the tide goes out, the snails and
limpets cling to the rocks. Barnacles and
mussels close their shells up tight. Crabs
and starfish look for hiding places and
wait for the next high tide.

 Seaweed

Seaweeds live along rocky shores.
These plants do not have roots because
there is no soil for them to dig into.
Instead, holdfasts at the base of their stem
grip tightly to the rocks.

Seaweeds bend with the water. So they
don't get damaged by the waves, tides and
currents. Some have gas-filled swellings,
to keep them afloat in the water.

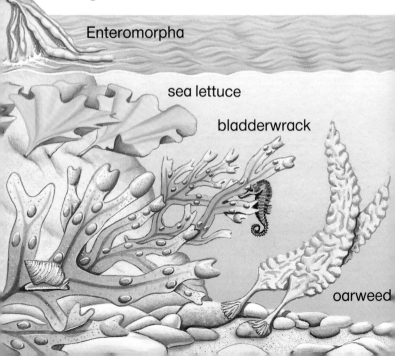

Enteromorpha

sea lettuce

bladderwrack

oarweed

Seaweeds live at different depths in the water. Sea lettuce lives in shallow water, where it is often exposed to air. Giant kelp forms dense forests in deep water.

Many animals live among the seaweeds. Snails and sea urchins graze seaweed for food. Some fish lay their eggs on seaweed, so they can hatch safely. Seals and sea otters hide in the kelp forests.

giant kelp

🐚 In the sand

On sandy shores, the wind often blows the sand into small hills called dunes. Grasses grow on the dunes and hold them in place.

dunes

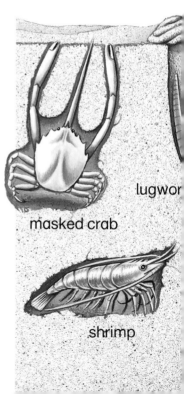

masked crab

lugwor

shrimp

60

long the beach animals burrow in the sand
protect themselves when the tide is out.

ome shellfish use a kind of foot to dig
hemselves into the sand. Razorshell clams
ave a large foot and a narrow shell, so
hey can bury themselves quickly. When
he tide is in, these shellfish stick out tubes
alled siphons and suck in seawater. The
ater contains tiny bits of food.

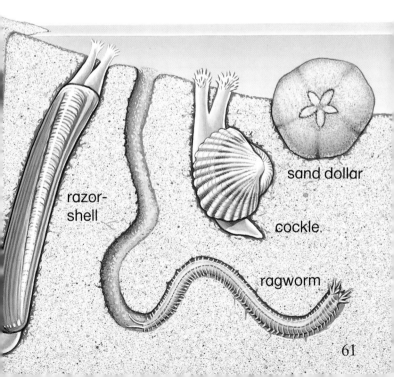

razor-
shell

sand dollar

cockle.

ragworm

🐚 Estuaries and deltas

An estuary is the wide mouth of a riv[er] where it meets the sea. Some rivers carry huge amount[s] of sand and mud down to the shore and dump it there. So the shore builds out into the sea. Th[is] is called deposition.

hen a river dumps sand and mud faster
an the ocean carries it away, a delta forms.

delta is low-lying land shaped a bit like
triangle. The top of the triangle starts at
e river mouth. As the river dumps more
diment, the delta grows wider. The river
is to divide into several channels to flow
rough the delta and reach the sea.

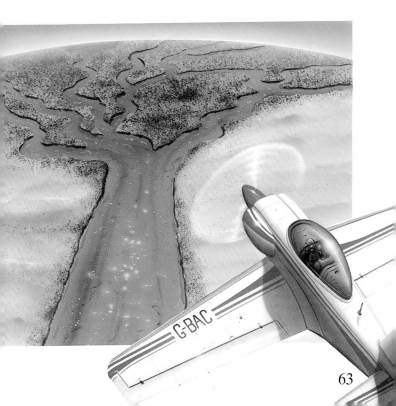

On the mudflats

In estuaries and deltas, the amount of sal
in the water constantly changes. When th
tide is in, the mudflats are flooded with
salty seawater. When the tide is out, only
fresh river water flows through.
The plants and animals here have to cope
with both types of water.

curlew   oystercatche

Birds use their beaks to poke into the mu
to find worms and other animals that bur
themselves in the mud.

It's easy to see why this bird is called a stilt!

With its long legs and long pointed beak, it can wade through the water and probe the mud for food.

stilt

redshank   turnstone

ome animals are buried deeper than
hers. Birds have beaks that are especially
ited for finding the food they eat.

🐚 Marshes and swamps

Where land meets ocean, there are sometimes soggy pieces of land called marshes and swamps. Marshes have no trees. Swamps do.

In marshes the roots of grasses and other plants trap sediment and stop it being washed away by the sea.

angrove trees
ow in tropical
amps. Their long
ots arch high above
e mud. Roots anchor
e tree in the mud, and
ey keep the rest of the tree
ove water, even at high tide.
he roots also help build up the
ast, because they trap sediment.

Amazing facts

Some sand is made not of rock but of pieces of shells ground up by the waves.

On some coasts, 70 pairs of guillemot nest together in just one square metre. That's about the same amount of space as an armchair!

Sea urchins eat kelp. Sea otters feed on the urchins and protect the kelp from being destroyed.

The Mississippi Delta is growing out into the Gulf of Mexico at the rate of 96 metres every year.

Deltas were named after the letter d or delta in the Greek alphabet, because that letter is shaped like a triangle.

The open

sea

Ocean zones

There are four main depth zones in the ocean. Different types of animals live in each zone.

The shallowest zone is called the epipelagic zone. Sunlight warms the water in this zone, and many plants live here. So many animals live here too, because they feed on the plants.

The next zone is called the mesopelagic zone. Sunlight barely reaches this far down, so plants cannot grow here. The animals living here must swim up to the epipelagic zone at night to feed.

In the bathypelagic and the really deep abyssopelagic zones, it is pitch dark. Very few animals live here. They must work hard to find food. Some eat particles of food which drift down from above. Some are skilful hunters.

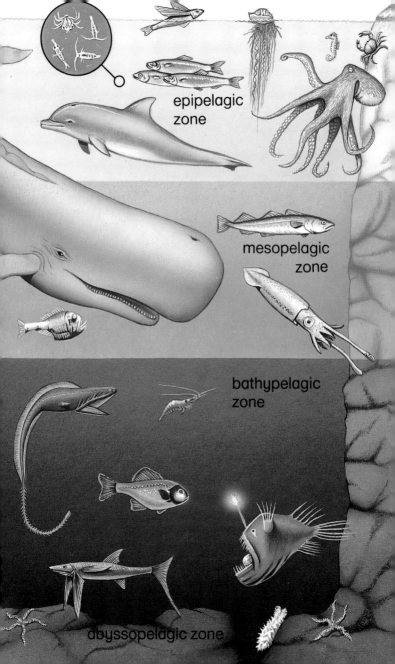

epipelagic
zone

mesopelagic
zone

bathypelagic
zone

abyssopelagic zone

 Plankton

The most important living things in the oceans are also the smallest. These are th plants and animals called plankton.

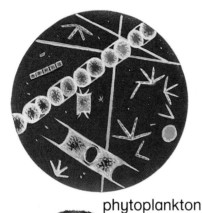

phytoplankton

zooplankt

Phytoplankton are plan Zooplankton are anima

Most plankton are so small that you can see them only with a microscope. There are millions of plankton in a jar of seawater.

Plankton are tiny, but they are food for many of the animals in the sea.

sea anemone

Sea anemones and corals on the seabed feed on plankton in shallow water.

Floating animals such as jellyfish feed on plankton. So do many fish such as mackerel.

jellyfish

mackerel

Blue whales, the largest animals in the ocean, feed on zooplankton called krill. One whale can eat four tonnes a day!

blue whale

Ocean food

Imagine animals and plants in the sea as links in a chain. They all need food.

Plants are at the end of the chain. They use sunlight as their food. Next are the small animals that feed on plants. Then there are the animals that eat them.

After that, there is an even larger animal hunting for its food.

harbour seal

killer whale

The hunters are called predators The victims are called prey.

ifferent animals
ed on different
ings. So there are
ousands of different
od chains in the oceans.
ne is shown here.

phytoplankton

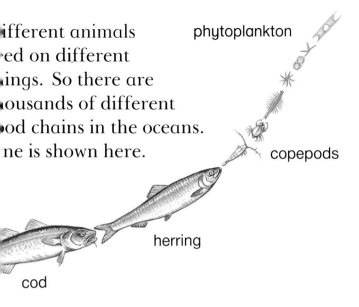

copepods

herring

cod

othing is wasted in the oceans. Animal
roppings, and dead animals and plants,
re broken down by tiny bacteria. This
releases minerals. The minerals help to
ourish the phytoplankton.

bacteria
(seen through a
powerful microscope)

Staying alive

To survive in the ocean an animal must find food, and it must avoid being eaten.

The octopus squirts a jet of dark ink to confuse predators. Then the octopus darts away and hides.

The sea dragon looks like a piece of seaweed. So it's hard to see.

Sea urchins protect themselves with spines that make them difficult to eat.

he Portuguese man-
-war has trailing
ntacles up to 12
etres long.
heir sting can be
poisonous as
cobra bite.

The clown fish is safe among the stinging tentacles of sea anemones. It does not get stung – but predators do. The anemones get scraps from the fish's meals.

🐟 Safety in numbers

Many sea creatures travel together in large groups called schools or shoals, to protect themselves.

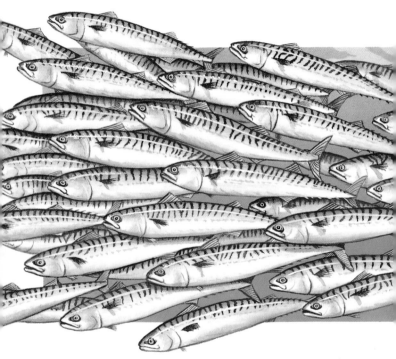

A huge school of fish confuses predators and makes it difficult for them to pick out just one to eat. But that is not enough to protect these mackerel from a barracuda.

arracudas are often called "the tigers of
e sea", because they are fierce hunters.
he biggest barracudas are almost two
etres long. They are fast swimmers.

o catch their prey, barracudas race
rough schools of fish and attack them
th snapping bites. You can see that a
rracuda has a mouthful of sharp teeth.

 A fish

There are about 13,000 different types, or species, of fish living in the oceans. This one is a goldfish.

Fish use their fins to help them swim through the water. The tail fin is waved from side to side to push the fish forward.

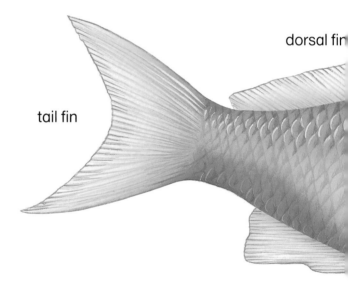

dorsal fin

tail fin

Other fins help the fish to stay upright and to change direction.

'e breathe in
xygen from the
r. Fish get their
xygen from the
ater.

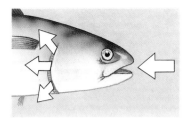

fish has gills, hidden behind gill slits on
ther side of its head. Water comes in
rough the fish's mouth. The gills take in
xygen from the water. Then the water
es out through the gill slits.

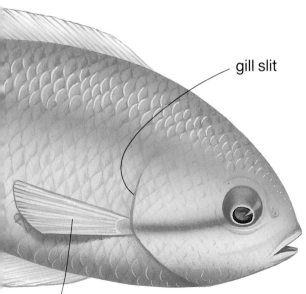

gill slit

pectoral fin

🐟 Ocean giants

Whales, dolphins and porpoises are not fish. They are mammals. Fish lay eggs. But whales, dolphins and porpoises give birth to their babies and feed them with their own milk – just as other mammals d

Fish have gills to take oxygen from the water. Whales, dolphins and porpoises have lungs, so they must rise to the surfac for air. They breathe in and out through blow-hole on the top of their heads.

blow-hole

maller whales,
ich as killer
hales, have teeth.
ut the largest
hales, including
umpback whales,
ave no teeth.

istead, they have thin strips of baleen.
he whale takes a huge gulp of water,
id strains it out again through the
ileen. The baleen traps the plankton, like
giant sieve. Baleen whales eat tonnes of
ankton a day.

 Sea sounds

Below the surface the oceans are full of noisy animals. Dolphins and whales give off a series of clicks. These sounds bounce back off other animals like an echo.

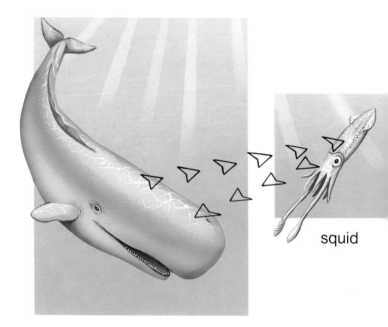

squid

The echoes help dolphins and whales to find their prey. Sperm whales can find squid up to 400 metres away.

olphins and
hales also
roduce clicks and
histles and other
unds to
mmunicate with
e another.

ientists record these sounds.
ut they do not understand
hale language yet.

umpback whales sing
ngs that last up to
minutes.
ut no one
ows why.

 # Sea journeys

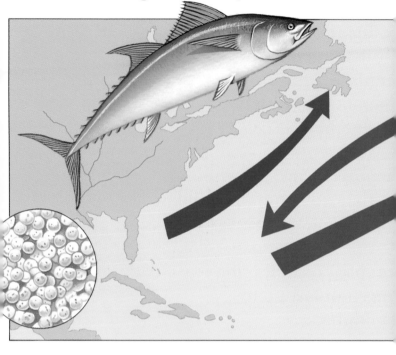

Many sea creatures regularly make long
journeys. These are called migrations.
Bluefin tuna lay their eggs in the warm
waters of the Caribbean Sea. Then they
migrate north across the Atlantic Ocean,
Nova Scotia. On the way they find lots
to eat, and nearly double their weight.

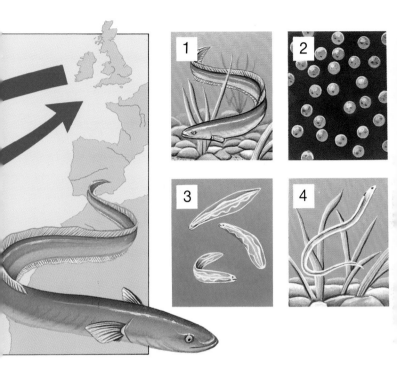

ome eels make an even longer journey.
hey leave their rivers in Europe and swim
cross the Atlantic Ocean to the Sargasso
ea near Bermuda, to lay their eggs.
he eggs hatch and the young eels travel
the Gulf Stream current all the way back
the rivers in Europe.

In the dark

The deep ocean is very cold, no warmer than three degrees Celsius, and very dark. There is not much food, so few animals live here. Those that do are often very small. They can survive on little food. Some of them eat only once every few months.

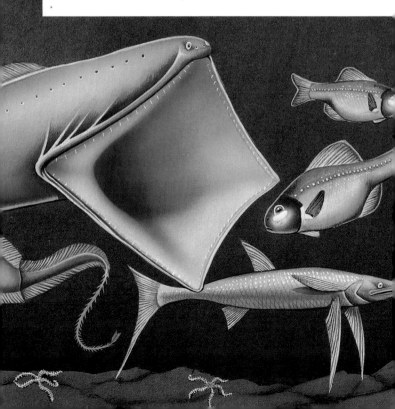

The gulper eel has jaws that open wide to gulp its prey. The angler fish waves a glowing lure to attract prey into its mouth. Flashlight fish light up parts of their bodies to signal to one another. Down on the seabed, tripod fish use their long fins like three stilts.

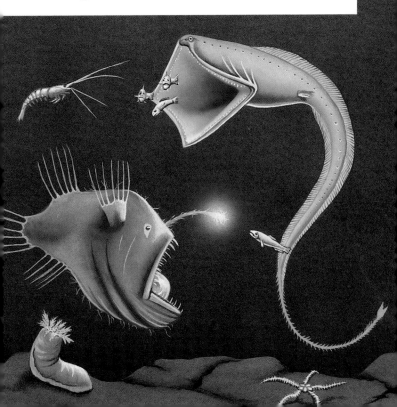

Amazing facts

The name plankton comes from the Greek word for wandering. Plankton cannot swim – they drift wherever the currents take them.

In an emergency most fish can swim ten times their body length in one second.

The stonefish which lives among coral reefs in the Indian and Pacific Oceans is deadly. A sting from the poisonous spines on its fins can kill a person in a few hours.

The blue whale is the largest animal that has ever lived. It can be up to 30 metres long and weigh up to 150 tonnes. That is as long as six elephants and as heavy as 22 elephants.

A school of whales or seals is called a pod. Killer whales go hunting in pods of up to 20 animals.

Ocean

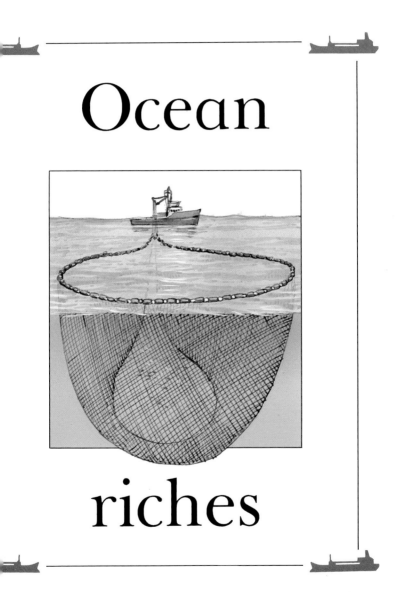

riches

Treasure from the sea

The oceans are full
of treasure.
You can collect
beautiful shells on
the beach.

Divers find pearls
inside oyster shells

Deep down on the
seafloor, there are
lumps of valuable
minerals. These
lumps are called
nodules.

y studying shipwrecks and their cargo on
e seabed, divers and scientists learn a lot
out how people lived long ago.

⛴ Looking for fish

Around the world, fishermen catch more than 70 million tonnes of food from the sea every year.

Fishermen find fish with the help of sonar. In the ship's hull, a machine called an echo-sounder sends out beeps of sound through the water. It measures the time it takes for the echoes to bounce back from the seabed. If a large shoal of fish gets in the way, the echo bounces back in a short time. The fisherman sees this on a screen.

atellites orbiting the Earth can help too.
'hey recognize the blue-green colour of
ie phytoplankton which fish eat. They
ieasure the amounts of blue and green
ght reflected from the ocean surface and
eam pictures back to Earth. Fishermen
now that where there are lots of phyto-
lankton there are likely to be lots of fish.

⬚ The catch

Fishermen use different nets to catch different fish. Long drift nets hang like a curtain from floats on the surface. Purse seine nets trap fish in a giant net bag. These nets catch herring, mackerel and other fish which swim near the surface.

 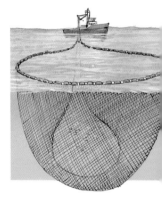

Boats drag trawling nets to catch cod and other fish which live near the seabed.

The nets are hauled
in. The crew sort the
fish, clean them and
pack them in ice to
keep them fresh.

⛴ Farming the sea

The oceans are so vast that it is easy to imagine they are a never-ending source o food. But this is not true.

Catching too many fish in one place mean there are not enough fish left behind to lc eggs. And *that* means not enough fish for the future.

too many fish today...

...not enough in futu

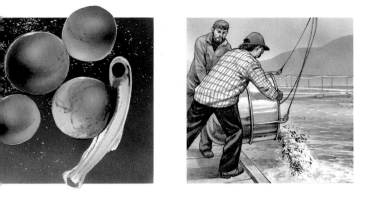

ish farms help provide fish for the future.
t the farm, fish hatch from eggs in tanks
f water. The young fish are kept in tanks
ntil they are big enough to be sold and
aten. Or they are put back into the sea.

eople farm other types of seafood too,
uch as mussels and edible seaweed.

ussels   seaweed

Mining the sea

One treasure from the sea is so common that we often forget about it. Everyone needs salt, and one way to get it is to use seawater.

In dry, sunny places, seawater is trapped in shallow ponds called salt pans. The he of the sun evaporates the water, and leav the salt behind.

il and gas are buried deep beneath the
afloor. Oil rigs drill a narrow hole down
the oil and gas and pump it up to the
arface. Tankers carry it all ashore, to
fineries. So do underwater pipelines.

efineries turn oil and gas into many
seful products, including petrol for cars
nd fuel to heat our homes.

⛴ Ocean power

Oil and gas will not last for ever, so people are looking for new sources of energy.

A power station in Norway uses waves to generate electricity. Waves push seawater up a special channel into a reservoir. The trapped water spins machines called turbines. The turbines generate electricity.

In France, engineers have built a tidal barrage across the mouth of the River Rance. Inside the barrage, turbines generate electricity when they are spun round by seawater. What happens? When the tide goes out, seawater pushes through the turbines and makes them spin. When the tide comes in, the turbines spin the other way.

Scientists and engineers are still experimenting with waves and tides.

More research will have to be done before these ideas work well enough to become useful sources of energy.

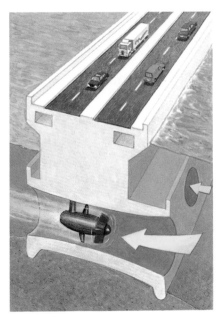

Amazing facts

Pearl divers used to hold their breath when they swam under water to collect th oysters. Most pearl divers were women, because women can stay under water longer than men without breathing. Now divers often have wet suits and tanks of a

Lumps of copper and other precious minerals lie deep down on the seafloor. But one day it may be possible to collect these nodules.

In some hot, dry countries such as Saudi Arabia, fresh water is very scarce. Desalination is a process that removes the salt from seawater to make fresh water fo people to drink.

The giant Californian kelp can grow 60 centimetres in one day and reaches 60 metres in length. This seaweed can provide methane gas for fuel.

People and

the sea

🤿 Studying the oceans

Oceanographers study the oceans.
They used to drop nets and simple
measuring tools over the side of a ship.

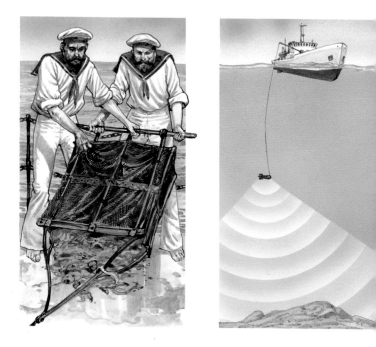

Now oceanographers can also explore the
deep with sonar. GLORIA is one echo-
sounding system. It measures sound waves
to give a clear picture of the sea floor.

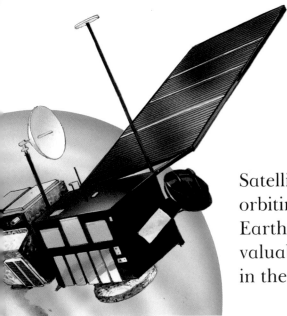

Satellites orbiting the Earth are valuable "eyes in the sky".

atellites send out radio waves and
leasure how they echo off the oceans.

his gives scientists
1formation about
1e shape of the
eafloor, the
attern of the
urrents, and the
emperature of
1e water.

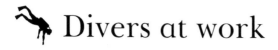 Divers at work

Divers carry out many important building and repair jobs to underwater pipelines, cables and oil rigs. They also explore the seabed for wrecks and wildlife.

wet suit

tank

mas

cam

Divers use scuba equipment for shallow dives of less than 50 metres. There is no air under water. So they carry air or a mixture of gases in a tank on their back.

For deeper dives, people wear diving suits made out of strong metal. Air is pumped down in a hose from a boat on the surface.

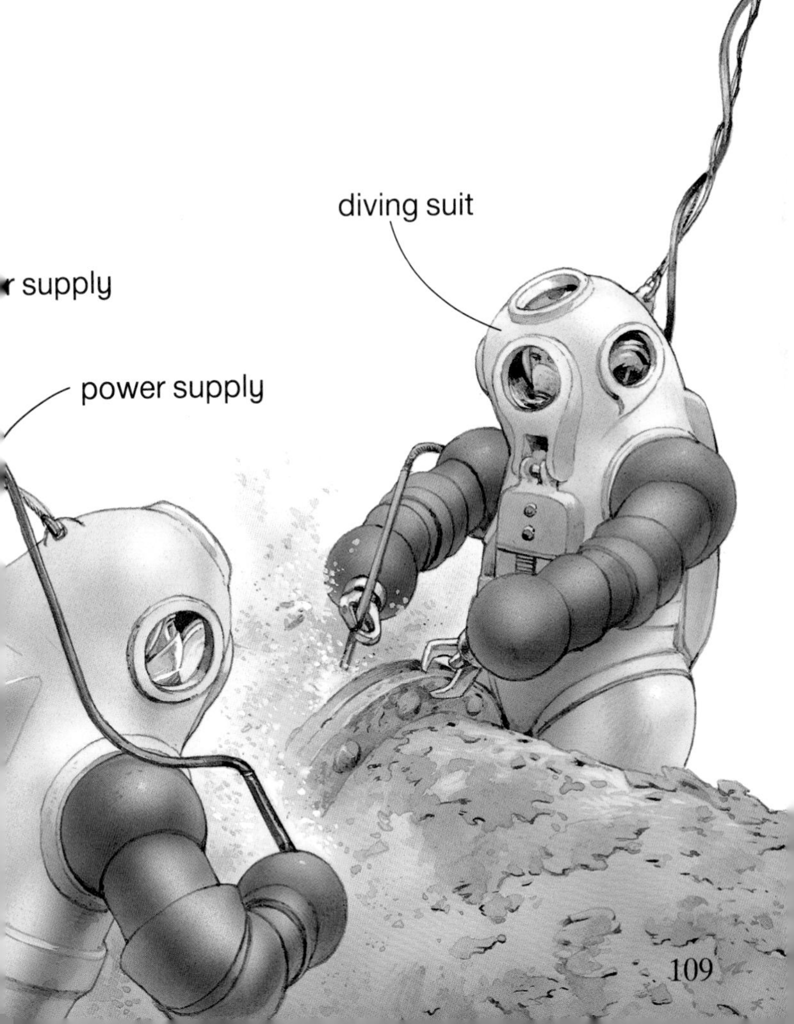

diving suit

supply

power supply

Going down

Underwater craft called submersibles take
people to the deepest parts of the ocean.

A mini-sub is launched from a ship at sea.
During the trip the mini-sub crew keeps in
touch with the ship by radio. They can
work under water for up to eight hours.
Then they return to the surface.

or very deep and dangerous dives, remote operated vehicles (ROVs) need no crew. They are controlled by a command cable from a support ship on the surface.

Some ROVs have robot arms that can hold cameras and tools to carry out inspections and repairs.

This ROV is scraping algae and shells off the steel legs of an oil rig.

 # Crossing the seas

Shipping lanes are like highways across th water, for ships carrying goods from one port to another.

ferry

container ship

Different ships carry different cargo. Huge tankers carry oil. Bulk carriers carry grain and other dry cargo. Some ships carry their cargo in containers. Ferries carry people, cars and trucks.

tanker   bulk carrier

Fun at the seaside

The sea is a wonderful place to have fun. Lifeguards and signs tell you when it is safe to go into the water. The best beaches are clean beaches.

Spoiling the sea

When people dump waste into the sea, they are polluting or dirtying the water.

Pollution harms the plants and animals that live in the sea.

Some factories let poisonous waste flow into rivers and down to the sea. Farm fertilizers and pesticides also seep into the oceans. Many of them harm sea life.

Sometimes the sea is used as a rubbish dump. Towns and cities pump sewage through pipelines into the sea. Barges tow rubbish out to sea to get rid of it.

Oil spills from tankers can kill thousands of birds and other animals in the sea.

When the oil is washed ashore by tides and currents, it ruins our beaches too. It takes a lot of hard work to clean up the coastline after an oil spill.

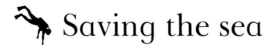

Saving the sea

The oceans are beautiful, and they are valuable. Everyone should do all they can to help protect them.

Conservation groups such as Friends of the Earth and Greenpeace try to protect the oceans. But there is still a lot to do.

What can you do?

ou could start by cleaning up your local
each. When you visit the seashore you
ould make sure you and your friends do
ot leave rubbish behind.

Best of all, you could learn
more about the sea. Then
you will know how to
protect it.

Amazing facts

In 1960 two people travelled to the bottom of the deepest ocean trench, almost 11 kilometres down, in a submersible called a bathyscaphe.

One of the most famous research submersibles is called Alvin. In 1986 it took pictures of the Titanic, a shipwreck lying 3,800 metres below the surface in the Atlantic.

The shipping lanes around north-western Europe are very crowded. Every week ships make more than 12,000 journeys there.

In 1989 the oil tanker Exxon Valdez hit some rocks in Alaska and spilled 44 million litres of oil. A stretch of coastline 1,200 kilometres long was covered with oil. Thousands of birds and fish were killed.

INDEX